Too Much Stuff!

Richard Cohen
Illustrated by Caroline Hu

Rigby®

A Harcourt Achieve Imprint

www.Rigby.com
1-800-531-5015

Literacy by Design Leveled Readers: *Too Much Stuff!*

ISBN-13: 978-1-4189-3667-9
ISBN-10: 1-4189-3667-7

Printed in China
3 4 5 6 7 8 985 14 13 12 11 10 09 08

Contents

Chapter One
This Place Is a Mess!

"I can't find anything around here!" Yolanda's dad complained while looking in the cabinets. "I need measuring cups to mix my pancake batter, but all I see are jars, pots, pans, and spoons."

As Dad began moving things around, Yolanda and her brother Anthony heard a loud noise. When they spun around to see what had happened, everything began tumbling out of the cabinets.

Crash! Clank! Clunk!

"Finally, the measuring cups!" Dad exclaimed. "Now I can make pancakes." Yolanda and Anthony just shook their heads and went back to reading their books.

After breakfast Yolanda's mom went into her home office to pay some bills, but she couldn't find a pen anywhere. She could find pencils, paper, and stamps, but not a pen. Papers were stacked in huge piles, and it looked like computer wires were attacking her desk.

"How can I work like this?" she asked herself. "When did my desk get so messy?"

In another part of the house, Anthony stood in his bedroom looking at the socks, shirts, and pants that covered the floor. Old toys spilled from the closet, and in the middle of the room there was a half-built rocket. He was making it for the science fair, but he kept losing things. He couldn't find the glue or an important chunk of the rocket's nose.

"There's nowhere for me to work," he complained to himself.

Yolanda was in her room, thinking about the sleepover she was planning. She would invite her best friends, Jenny and Rosa.

Frowning, she thought, "How can I have a sleepover if there is no place for anyone to sleep?" Old stuffed animals, CDs, books, and clothing covered every inch of her floor.

Even the family cat, Sport, was feeling the space crunch. He couldn't find a comfortable place to curl up for a nap. In Sport's favorite spot by the fireplace, Dad was repairing an old computer.

"We have to do something about this! Our house has gotten completely out of control!" Yolanda declared. "I'm going to call a family meeting."

Chapter Two
The Family Meeting

At the meeting Mom said, "Maybe we should sell this house and buy something bigger."

"No!" Yolanda and Anthony said at the same time. They loved the small, old house they had grown up in.

"Maybe we should have a garage sale and get rid of the stuff we don't need," Dad suggested.

Everyone thought a garage sale was a great idea.

"I'll need some time, though, to get my stuff organized," Mom said.

"OK," Yolanda said eagerly, "and if we all clean out our own areas and put our stuff in boxes, I'll run the garage sale. I'll put price labels on the items, set them out, meet the customers, and collect all of the money."

"I want to do that, too!" Anthony whined.

"You can both do it," Dad said. "If you work together, you can split the money."

"Half of what each of you makes will have to go into your savings accounts," said Mom. "The other half is yours to spend."

With smiles on their faces, Yolanda and Anthony shook hands. Then they all went to their rooms and began sorting.

Yolanda got four big boxes, one for each family member to use. She wrote a name on each box and put the boxes in the garage. All morning she worked in her bedroom sorting through old books, clothes, stuffed animals, and toys. It was hard for her to say goodbye to the objects she used to love, but she knew she had to do it if she wanted to make some money and have her slumber party.

Grunting and sputtering, Yolanda carried two bags filled with her things to the garage. She dumped the contents into her box, and then she peeked curiously into the other three boxes. They were all empty!

"Am I the only one around here doing any work?" she thought.

Yolanda called the family together for another meeting.

"What is going on?" she demanded.

"It's hard to get rid of things," Mom admitted, laughing. "I have three old coats I know I should sell, but I can't bring myself to put them in that box."

"And I have model kits I'll never build," Dad said, "but, well, maybe someday I'll build them."

"And I have toys that I just can't give up," said Anthony.

Chapter Three
No One Will Notice

"We'll never have a garage sale if we all think this way," Yolanda pointed out.

"You're probably right," Anthony murmured softly.

"Wow, I can't remember the last time I heard you say that your sister was right!" Dad exclaimed.

"I know," Anthony said, "so this time you can be sure she's right!"

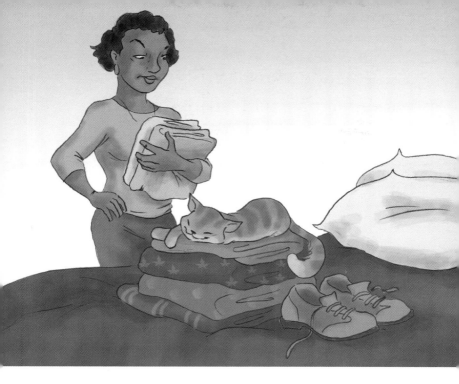

They all went back to their areas and started over again. Mom piled together the clothes and shoes she never wore anymore. Dad lumped together the kits he thought he would never finish and the broken things he would never fix. Anthony chose the toys he no longer played with, as well as some clothes he never wore.

Yolanda finished filling another bag with things to sell and, humming happily, she went downstairs and dumped her stuff into the box. This time, the other three boxes were full.

She peered into Anthony's box just to see what he had decided to sell. Sticking out of his pile was the sleeve of an old, fuzzy, gray sweatshirt.

Yolanda grabbed the sweatshirt out of her brother's box.

"This is a great sweatshirt!" she exclaimed as she tried it on. "I wonder why Anthony would get rid of this. If he didn't want it, he could have just given it to me."

She went upstairs wearing the sweatshirt, thinking that no one would notice.

As Anthony brought another bag to the garage, his eyes lit up when he saw an old, beat-up kit spilling out from his father's box. *Build Your Own Model Jet Plane!* was written on the kit in bold letters.

"That sounds interesting," he thought. Softly, he tiptoed upstairs with the kit under his shirt, thinking that no one would notice.

Later in the day, Dad clopped downstairs carrying another bag. He decided to take a peek in his wife's box. Digging around inside it, he uncovered a small, steel box with a metal lock. "This would be perfect for keeping addresses and notes in!" he thought. Carrying the metal box behind his back, he went upstairs as quietly as he could, thinking that no one would notice.

Soon after, Mom walked downstairs bringing her next bag of things. While she was there, she decided to peek into Dad's box and found a pair of red woolen gloves.

She put the soft gloves on her hands, and admired them as she rushed up the creaking wooden stairs, thinking that no one would notice.

That evening Yolanda visited

Anthony's room to see how well
he was cleaning up. She found him
sitting on the floor with a tube of
glue, building a model jet plane.

"Isn't that Dad's?" she asked. "He
said he was going to sell all of his
old model kits!"

"It is Dad's, but . . . isn't that my
old sweatshirt?"

"Oops," said Yolanda, looking
down at what she was wearing.
"I forgot to take it off."

"I guess it's time for another
family meeting," said Anthony.

Chapter Four
Kids at Work

"OK, everybody, fess up," Yolanda said at the meeting that evening. "I took this gray sweatshirt from Anthony's box, and he took something from Dad's box."

Giggling, Mom and Dad showed Yolanda and Anthony the red gloves and the steel box they had taken from each other's garage sale objects.

"It's no wonder we have so much clutter in this house!" Mom said, laughing.

During the following week, the whole family began cleaning their rooms again and filling the boxes for the garage sale. This time, they made sure not to take back anything once it had gone into a box. It worked! Yolanda now had plenty of space for a sleepover, and Anthony had room to build his rocket. Mom could find things on her desk again, and Dad could play with his models and cook wonderful breakfasts without spilling things all over the floor.

Yolanda and Anthony went into the garage and saw the boxes piled high with items to sell.

"Come on, Anthony, let's get started!" Yolanda said.

"You mean there's more that we have to do?" Anthony asked.

"Are you kidding? We have to sort everything into piles: clothes in one spot, toys in another, and so on."

"I didn't know what I was getting into!" Anthony moaned.

Anthony and Yolanda spent all day together sorting the items. They divided the clothes into four separate groups: men's, women's, girls', and boys'. They stacked the books and records and made separate piles for toys, games, kitchen tools, garden tools, and workshop tools.

"Well, I guess we're ready for the sale, huh?" Anthony said.

"Not yet!" Yolanda replied. "Now we have to make everything look nice. We need to hang the clothes on hangers. We need to set up some tables to put books and other things on, and we need to put a price label on everything."

"Are you sure you're not just making this all up so you can boss me around more?" Anthony asked.

"I'm not bossy!" Yolanda said. "I just like things to be done the right way, that's all."

"Well, why are you always the one who knows the right way?"

"I'm older than you," Yolanda said with a sniff. "You want to make money, don't you?"

"All right, all right, where do we start?" asked Anthony.

Chapter Five
What a Sale!

The day before the sale, Yolanda and Anthony made signs and posted them around the neighborhood. A neighbor walking her dog read the sign and said, "I'll be there!"

"That's great!" said Yolanda. "We have a lot of things to sell!"

On the day of the sale, the weather was perfect. Yolanda and Anthony moved some of the things outside onto the driveway to make more room for customers to walk around and browse. All day long, cars stopped by and parked outside the family's house. It seemed as if people from all over the neighborhood came by to see what was for sale.

A boy in Anthony's class bought an old cell phone for just twenty-five cents.

"I'm going to take it apart and see how it works for my science fair project," he told Yolanda.

A woman down the street bought an old hand mixer and a set of dessert bowls.

Yolanda even made a new friend at the sale. A tall girl she had never seen before was looking at a model boat kit. The girl took it out of the box and looked at the pieces for the sails.

"Wow, I wish I could build this," the girl said longingly.

"You can, for just one dollar!" Yolanda said with delight.

"We just moved into this neighborhood," the girl's mom said. "This is Rachel!"

"Maybe when I start building this boat, you can help, OK?" Rachel said to Yolanda.

"That would be great!" Yolanda said.

It was exciting to sell things, talk to new people, and hand them their change. By the end of the day, almost all of the items had been sold.

"Maybe when I grow up, I'll start a chain of resale stores!" thought Yolanda.

When the sun started setting, Yolanda and Anthony put the items they didn't sell into the empty boxes to give away to charity. They folded most of the tables and leaned them against the garage wall. They swept the driveway, picked up all of the trash, and then finally sat down and counted the money. They had made two hundred dollars!

"We knew you could do it!"
Mom said, hugging them both.
"Remember that you'll each need
to put fifty dollars in your savings
accounts."

"We know," said Anthony and
Yolanda wisely.

Chapter Six
The Sleepover

Two weeks later, Yolanda had her sleepover. She invited Jenny and Rosa—and her new friend Rachel. Jenny brought a red and blue checked sleeping bag that she had bought at the garage sale, Rosa brought a word game that she had bought at the sale, and Rachel brought the model boat for them all to work on together.

"It's great that our old stuff found new homes!" Yolanda said proudly.

The sale had been a great success, and the grown-ups were still talking about it when they picked the girls up at Yolanda's house the next morning.

"I want to have a garage sale," Rosa's mom said. "We have an attic full of things we never use."

"We have lots of kitchen stuff to sell," said Jenny's mom. "Why don't we have a two-family sale?"

"Kitchen stuff?" Yolanda's dad exclaimed. "I'm always looking for old gadgets, and now that we've cleaned up, there is plenty of room to add to my collection!"

Yolanda, Anthony, and Mom rolled their eyes at each other and laughed.

"Please, Dad," Yolanda begged, "not again!"